GREECE

EXPLORE THE COUNTRIES · EXPLORE THE COUNTRIES · EXPLORE THE COUNTRIES · EXPLORE THE COUNTRIES

Big Buddy Books

An Imprint of Abdo Publishing
www.abdopublishing.com

Julie Murray

www.abdopublishing.com

Published by Abdo Publishing, a division of ABDO, PO Box 398166, Minneapolis, Minnesota 55439.
Copyright © 2015 by Abdo Consulting Group, Inc. International copyrights reserved in all countries. No part
of this book may be reproduced in any form without written permission from the publisher. Big Buddy Books™
is a trademark and logo of Abdo Publishing.

Printed in the United States of America, North Mankato, Minnesota.
032014
092014

THIS BOOK CONTAINS
RECYCLED MATERIALS

Cover Photo: iStockphoto.
Interior Photos: Anhaeuser/Giorgos Nikolaidis/picture-alliance/dpa/AP Images (p. 25), AFP/Getty Images
    (p. 23), ASSOCIATED PRESS (pp. 15, 19, 25, 33), Getty Images (p. 31), Glow Images (pp. 16, 21, 29),
    iStockphoto (p. 11), Popperfoto/Getty Images (p. 15), Shutterstock (pp. 5, 9, 11, 19, 27, 34, 35, 37, 38),
    Roger Viollet/Getty Images (p. 17), Bernd Weiëbrod/picture-alliance/dpa/AP Images (p. 13).

Coordinating Series Editor: Rochelle Baltzer
Editor: Sarah Tieck
Contributing Editors: Bridget O'Brien, Marcia Zappa
Graphic Design: Adam Craven

Country population and area figures taken from the CIA World Factbook.

Library of Congress Cataloging-in-Publication Data

Murray, Julie, 1969-
 Greece / Julie Murray.
    pages cm. -- (Explore the countries)
 ISBN 978-1-62403-342-1
1. Greece--Juvenile literature. I. Title.
 DF717.M87 2014
 949.5--dc23
                         2013051238

GREECE

CONTENTS

AROUND THE WORLD

Our world has many countries. Each country has beautiful land. It has its own rich history. And, the people have their own languages and ways of life.

Greece is a country in Europe. What do you know about Greece? Let's learn more about this place and its story!

Did You Know?

Greece's official language is Greek.

Greece is known for its islands and cliffs.

Passport to Greece

Greece is a country in southern Europe. Four countries border it. It is also bordered by three seas. Greece's total area is 50,949 square miles (131,957 sq km). About 10.8 million people live there.

WHERE IN THE WORLD?

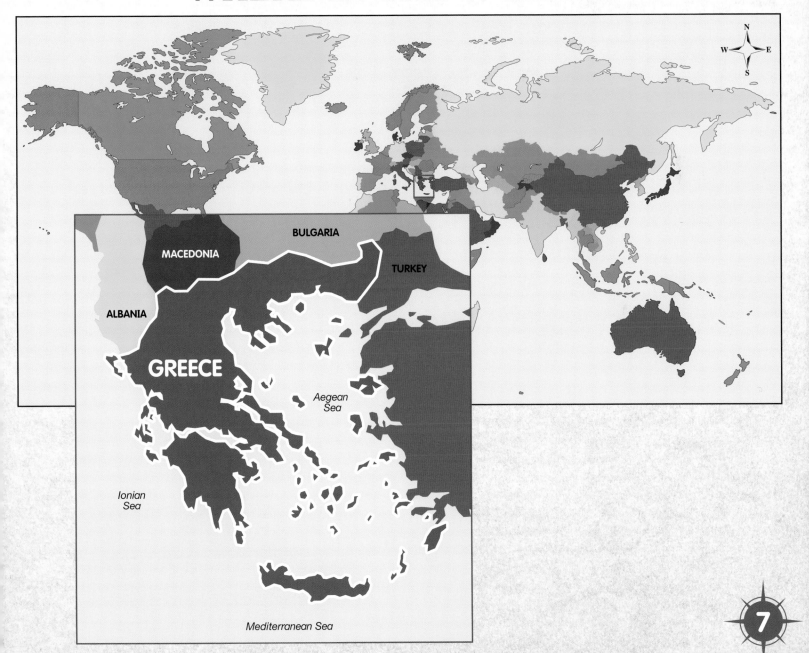

IMPORTANT CITIES

Athens is Greece's **capital** and largest city. More than 664,000 people live there. Many more live in nearby cities and towns.

Athens is known for its history and the arts. Many say it is where Western **civilization** began. Athens is home to important schools, such as the University of Athens.

Did You Know?

In 2004, Athens hosted the Olympic Games.

Athens is home to remains of buildings that are thousands of years old.

Thessaloníki is Greece's second-largest city. More than 315,000 people live there. Many more live in nearby areas. The city has a large port. Fruits, vegetables, and cotton ship from there.

Piraeus is another large city in Greece. It is home to more than 163,000 people. The city has three harbors and is the country's leading port.

SAY IT

Thessaloníki
theh-sah-loh-NEE-kee

Piraeus
peye-REE-uhs

Cloth, soap, and leather products are made in Thessaloníki's factories.

Piraeus has been an important port since the days of ancient Greece.

GREECE IN HISTORY

People have lived in Greece for more than 5,000 years. The first known **civilization** was a tribe called the Minoans. It started on the island of Crete. The people traded goods, made art, and built palaces.

The Mycenaeans took power around 1450 BC. They traded goods and created bronze objects. They also planned and built bridges and buildings.

SAY IT

Minoan
muh-NOH-uhn

Mycenaean
meye-suh-NEE-uhn

People are still able to see parts of Minoan buildings.

13

Beginning around 700 BC, Greeks lived in city-states. These small areas had their own governments.

Around 508 BC, Athens became the world's first known democracy. This type of government is ruled by the people.

Over the years, Greece was ruled by different groups. In 338 BC, the Macedonians took over. In 146 BC, the Romans gained power. Later, the land was part of the Ottoman **Empire**. Greece became independent in 1829.

Did You Know?

The first known Olympic Games were held in 776 BC in Olympia, Greece.

In the 400s BC, Athens was one of the world's most powerful cities. Famous thinkers such as Socrates (*right*) lived there.

TIMELINE

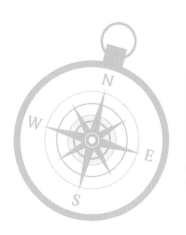

1588

El Greco of Crete completed the *Burial of the Count de Orgaz*. It is one of his most famous paintings.

About 460 BC

Hippocrates was born on the island of Cos. His new ideas changed the practice of **medicine**.

447–438 BC

The Parthenon was built. It became one of Greece's most famous buildings.

1829

The Greeks freed themselves from Ottoman rule. Athens became the new country's **capital** in 1933.

2013

Greece began to recover after a **recession** that started in 2009.

1896

The first modern Olympics were held in Athens. Before this, the ancient Greeks had held Olympic Games.

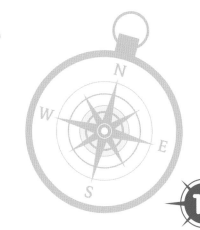

An Important Symbol

Greece's flag was first adopted in 1822. It has a white cross on a blue square in the top left corner. The flag also has nine blue and white stripes.

Greece's government is a **parliamentary republic**. A group called the Vouli makes laws. The prime minister is the head of government. The president is the head of state.

The cross on Greece's flag stands for the Greek Orthodox Church.

Karolos Papoulias became Greece's president in 2005.

Antonis Samaras became the prime minister in 2012.

ACROSS THE LAND

Greece is known for its beautiful, sunny land. Most parts of the country are near the sea, with mild weather. But in some areas, people ski on snowy slopes!

Much of the land in Greece is rocky. The country's main mountain range is the Pindus. Its highest point is Mount Olympus, at 9,570 feet (2,917 m). Greece also has **volcanoes**.

Volcanoes are found on the southern islands of Greece.

Did You Know?

In January, the average high temperature in Athens is about 55°F (13°C). In July, it is 89°F (32°C).

Many kinds of animals live in Greece. These include deer, boars, weasels, and foxes. There are pelicans, egrets, and storks. Turtles, fish, shrimp, and dolphins live in the water.

Greece's land is home to thousands of different plants. There are olive, cypress, chestnut, and fir trees. Oranges, dates, and figs grow there.

The dolphin is Greece's national animal.

23

Earning a Living

In Greece, most people have service jobs. Some work for the government or help the country's visitors. Others work in factories making goods. These include cement, cloth, and food and drinks.

Greece has some **natural resources**. Anchovies, mackeral, and sardines come from its waters. Farmers grow corn and wheat. They raise cattle, sheep, and goats.

Much fishing takes place in the Aegean Sea (*above*). The fish are then sold at markets (*left*).

SAY IT

Aegean
ih-JEE-uhn

LIFE IN GREECE

Some Greeks live on islands or in the countryside or mountains. But most people live in cities. Cities may be crowded. There are a mix of old and new buildings.

Greeks eat lamb, beef, chicken, pork, and seafood. They also eat fresh tomatoes and eggplant. Oregano, onions, and garlic are used to flavor Greek dishes.

Did You Know?

In Greece, children must attend school from ages 6 to 15.

Feta cheese is made from sheep's milk or goat's milk. It is popular in many Greek dishes. Olive oil and olives are also common.

Many Greeks enjoy soccer, basketball, and swimming. Folk dancing and folk music are popular. Weaving rugs and making jewelry are common art forms.

The Greek Orthodox Church is the country's official religion. The churches are known for their beauty.

Greek Orthodox churches are filled with art.

In Crete, weavers make beautiful patterned rugs.

Famous Faces

Plato was born in Athens around 427 BC. He was an important thinker, teacher, and writer.

Plato wrote 35 works and a group of letters. He shared ideas about the soul, art, and government. One of his most famous works is *The Republic*. He died around 347 BC. Today, people continue to read his ideas and writings.

Plato's writing and ideas changed the Western way of life.

Maria Callas was a world-famous opera singer. She was born in New York on December 2, 1923. Her parents were Greek.

In 1937, Callas and her parents returned to Greece. She studied music there. She first sang at the Athens Opera at age 17.

Callas went on to sing all over the world. She was known for her high voice. Callas died in 1977.

Opera singers are known for their powerful voices and beautiful costumes.

TOUR BOOK

Imagine traveling to Greece! Here are some places you could go and things you could do.

Explore

Play in the waves on Myrtos Beach on the island of Kefalonia. This beach is known for its colorful water.

Learn

Visit the theater of ancient Delphi. It could once seat 5,000 people. Today, it is popular with visitors.

 ## Walk

Visit Santorini and wander down the cobblestone streets. This island has beautiful views of the water.

Discover

Many people hike in the Samariá gorge in Crete. There are pine and cypress forests as well as mountain cliffs.

 ## See

The Parthenon is a Greek temple. It is more than 2,000 years old! It is on a hill above Athens.

A Great Country

The story of Greece is important to our world. Greece is a land of mountains and beaches. It is a country of great thinkers.

The people and places that make up Greece offer something special. They help make the world a more beautiful, interesting place.

Mount Athos is an area of the country with important religious buildings.

Greece Up Close

Official Name: Ellinikí Dhimokratía
(Hellenic Republic)

Flag:

Population (rank): 10,775,557
(July 2014 est.)
(81st most-populated country)

Total Area (rank): 50,949 square miles
(97th largest country)

Capital: Athens

Official Language: Greek

Currency: Euro

Form of Government: Parliamentary
republic

National Anthem: "Ymnos eis tin
Eleftherian" (Hymn to Liberty)

IMPORTANT WORDS

capital a city where government leaders meet.

civilization a well-organized and advanced society.

empire a large group of states or countries under one ruler called an emperor or empress.

medicine (MEH-duh-suhn) an item used in or on the body to treat an illness, ease pain, or heal a wound.

natural resources useful and valued supplies from nature.

parliamentary republic a government that has a leader who is usually a president, not a king or queen. It is run by a cabinet whose members belong to the legislature.

recession (rih-SEH-shuhn) a period of economic trouble. There is less buying and selling and people may be out of work.

volcano a deep opening in Earth's surface from which hot liquid rock or steam comes out.

WEBSITES

To learn more about Explore the Countries, visit **booklinks.abdopublishing.com**. These links are routinely monitored and updated to provide the most current information available.

INDEX